A Robbie Reader

What's So Great About...?

BARACK OBAMA

Claire O'Neal

South Huntington Pub. Lib.
145 Pidgeon Hill Rd.
Huntington Sta., N.Y. 11746

Mitchell Lane
PUBLISHERS
P.O. Box 196
Hockessin, Delaware 19707
Visit us on the web: www.mitchelllane.com
Comments? email us: mitchelllane@mitchelllane.com

PUBLISHERS

Copyright © 2010 by Mitchell Lane Publishers. All rights reserved. No part of this book may be reproduced without written permission from the publisher. Printed and bound in the United States of America.

Printing   1   2   3   4   5   6   7   8   9

A Robbie Reader
What's So Great About . . . ?

Amelia Earhart
Barack Obama
Daniel Boone
Elizabeth Blackwell
Galileo
Helen Keller
Johnny Appleseed
Martin Luther King Jr.
Pocahontas
Sam Houston

Anne Frank
The Buffalo Soldiers
Davy Crockett
Ferdinand Magellan
George Washington Carver
Henry Hudson
King Tut
Michelle Obama
Robert Fulton
The Tuskegee Airmen

Annie Oakley
Christopher Columbus
The Donner Party
Francis Scott Key
Harriet Tubman
Jacques Cartier
Lewis and Clark
Paul Bunyan
Rosa Parks

Library of Congress Cataloging-in-Publication Data
O'Neal, Claire.
  What's so great about Barack Obama / by Claire O'Neal.
    p. cm. — (A Robbie reade) (What's so great about . . . ?)
  Includes bibliographical references and index.
  ISBN 978-1-58415-830-1 (library bound)
 1. Obama, Barack—Juvenile literature. 2. Presidents—United States—Biography—Juvenile literature. 3. Racially mixed people—United States—Biography—Juvenile literature. I. Title.
  E908.O544 2010
  973.932092—dc22
  [B]

2009027358

ABOUT THE AUTHOR: A versatile author, Claire O'Neal has published several books with Mitchell Lane, in addition to professional scientific papers. She holds degrees in English and Biology from Indiana University, and a Ph.D. in Chemistry from the University of Washington. Claire now lives in Delaware, home of Vice President Joe Biden, with her husband, two young sons, and a fat black cat.

PUBLISHER'S NOTE: The following story has been thoroughly researched and to the best of our knowledge represents a true story. While every possible effort has been made to ensure accuracy, the publisher will not assume liability for damages caused by inaccuracies in the data, and makes no warranty on the accuracy of the information contained herein.

PLB

TABLE OF CONTENTS

Chapter One
A House Divided 5

Chapter Two
A Child of the World 9

Chapter Three
Sense of Responsibility 13

Chapter Four
A Political Star Is Born 17

Chapter Five
"Yes We Can" 21

Chronology 27
Timeline in History 28
Find Out More 29
    Books 29
    Works Consulted 29
    On the Internet 30
Glossary 31
Index 32

Words in **bold** type can be found in the glossary.

Senator Barack Obama announces his run for president to a crowd of supporters on February 10, 2007. As president, he said, he would pull U.S. troops out of Iraq and make health care available to every American. Though he had spent only two years in the U.S. Senate, he said, "I've been there long enough to know that the ways of Washington must change."

CHAPTER ONE

A House Divided

On February 10, 2007, U.S. Senator Barack Obama climbed the steps of the Old State Capitol in Springfield, Illinois, to announce that he would run for president of the United States. Obama chose this special place and day to remember his hero, Abraham Lincoln. Just like Obama, Lincoln was a lawyer. Both men served in the Illinois State Senate. Just like Obama, Lincoln had been new to national politics, serving only two years in the U.S. Senate, before running for president.

On the same steps in 1858, Lincoln spoke against slavery. He argued that slavery had ripped America apart, saying, "A house divided against itself cannot stand." In 2008, or 150 years later, the country was again divided. This time it had "red" states and "blue" states. In the

CHAPTER ONE

2004 presidential (preh-sih-DEN-shul) election, the red states had voted for Republican George W. Bush, and the blue states had voted for Democrat John Kerry.

In Obama's eyes, the red-blue division hurt America. Divided politicians avoided making tough decisions. He said they fought "instead of rolling up [their] sleeves . . . to tackle big problems." Many Americans agreed that the country had big problems. U.S. troops were fighting a war in Iraq that Obama had disagreed with all along. A growing number of Americans were beginning to disagree, too.

President Obama made a surprise trip to Camp Victory, a U.S. military base near Baghdad, Iraq, on April 7, 2009. He thanked soldiers there for their hard, selfless work in making Iraq a safer place.

Obama's presidential campaign called for "Change We Can Believe In." He asked voters to believe "not just in my ability to bring about real change in Washington. I'm asking you to believe in yours." He encouraged people to make America a better place by volunteering to help in their **communities** (kuh-MYOO-nih-teez).

Working families could not afford high gas prices, health care bills, and houses that cost more than they were worth.

Despite all the worry and disagreements, Obama had faith in the strength of the American people. "That's why this **campaign** can't only be about me," he said to the Springfield audience. "It must be about us—it must be about what we can do together . . . realizing that few **obstacles** can withstand the power of millions of voices calling for change."

CHAPTER TWO

A Child of the World

Barack Hussein Obama Jr. was born on August 4, 1961, in Honolulu, Hawaii. His mother was a white woman from Kansas named Stanley Ann Dunham. His father, Barack Sr., was a black exchange student from Kenya. They met as students at the University of Hawaii and married a few months later. In the 1960s, Barack's mixed-race background would have caused him problems in many states. But Hawaii was a melting pot of races, with white, Polynesian (pah-luh-NEE-jhun), Asian, and a few black families. He says, "That my father was black as **pitch**, my mother white as milk, barely registered in my mind."

When Barack, or "Barry," was two years old, his father left him and Ann to attend Harvard University. Ann raised Barry herself

9

CHAPTER TWO

while finishing her college degree. She taught him important values—to be honest, serve others, and always think the best of everyone. She told him to be proud of his black **heritage** (HAYR-ih-tidj). She read him Martin Luther King Jr.'s speeches and introduced him to the work of Lena Horne and other jazz musicians (myoo-ZIH-shuns).

Ann married Lelo Soetoro, who was from Indonesia (in-doh-NEE-jhuh), in 1966. The family moved to that country the next year. Barry's half sister, Maya, was born there in 1970.

Indonesia was **exotic** (ek-ZAH-tik)—Barry had a pet ape! But the country was also very poor. Ann worried that the schools there weren't the best choice for her son. In 1971, Barry won a **scholarship** (SKAH-lur-ship) to a private school in Hawaii. Ann tearfully sent him to live there with her parents.

Teachers at Punahou School in Hawaii remember Barry as bright and friendly, but a little lazy. He played on the basketball team but was never a star athlete. Though he had many

A CHILD OF THE WORLD

Obama (circled) with his fifth-grade class at Punahou School in Hawaii in 1972. His sister Maya told the *New York Times* that growing up in Hawaii "gave him a sense that a lot of different voices and textures can sort of live together, however imperfectly."

friends, he had no mother or father at home, and his mixed-race background made him feel lonely. He did not fit in with the small number of blacks on the island because of his white family. He stood out from his classmates because of his dark skin and curly hair. When he graduated in 1979, he looked beyond Hawaii for a place where he could belong.

A popular, thought-provoking professor, Obama taught at the University of Chicago for twelve years.

Obama with his grandparents, Stanley and Madelyn Dunham

CHAPTER THREE

Sense of Responsibility

At Occidental (ok-sih-DEN-tul) College in Los Angeles, Obama realized what he wanted to do. He wanted to act against poverty, prejudice, and injustice in Los Angeles and around the world. In his second year there, he protested with many others against **apartheid** (uh-PAR-tyd) in South Africa. "When he talked . . . people listened," schoolmate John Boyer told the *New York Times*. "He had a great sense of humor and could **diffuse** an argument."

Obama transferred to Columbia University in New York City, finishing his degree in political science in 1983. He studied constantly and read classic novels or **philosophy** (fih-LAH-suh-fee). He rented cheap apartments where gunshots could be heard in the night. He saw how hard it was for the poor in America,

CHAPTER THREE

especially **minorities** (my-NAHR-ih-teez), to get ahead. He vowed to use his skills for "helping the helpless and giving voice to the voiceless."

In 1985, Obama became a community organizer on the South Side of Chicago. For three years, he walked or drove the streets of run-down neighborhoods. He talked to residents about their needs and how to fill them. In his biggest triumph, Obama convinced the city to clean up a polluted housing project. The experience helped Obama find a place where his race was not a question. His actions for the people were welcome both on the streets and in city hall. He noticed that Harold Washington, Chicago's first black mayor, was a real agent of change. Inspired to run for office, Obama quit his job to pursue a law degree.

At Harvard Law School, Obama's experience and drive impressed his teachers. In 1990, Obama made national news when the *Harvard Law Review* elected Obama as its first black president. After only one year at Harvard, he landed a summer **internship** (IN-turn-ship) at the Chicago law firm of Sidley Austin. There

SENSE OF RESPONSIBILITY

Obama fell for the smart, funny Michelle right away. He asked her out many times before she finally said yes. For their first date, he took her out for an ice cream cone and a movie—Spike Lee's, *Do the Right Thing*. They were married two years later.

he worked for Michelle Robinson, another brilliant young black lawyer who had graduated from Harvard Law. Michelle and Barack married in Chicago in 1992.

15

Obama works behind his state senate desk in Springfield, Illinois.

Hoping to win a U.S. Senate seat, Obama delivers a memorable speech at the Democratic National Convention on July 27, 2004.

CHAPTER FOUR

A Political Star Is Born

The people of Chicago elected Barack Obama to the Illinois State Senate in 1996. He spent eight years there, writing laws that provided health care for the poor, improved prisons, and kept political campaigns honest. Meanwhile, he helped Michelle raise their two daughters, Malia Ann (born in 1998) and Natasha, called Sasha (born in 2001). Obama made a difference in the state senate, but he felt he could do more at the national level.

In 2000, Obama campaigned to be U.S. Representative, but Bobby Rush easily beat him. When a U.S. Senate seat needed filling in 2004, Obama saw his second chance. That race drew national attention, especially toward the young, exciting Obama. In a stirring speech at the Democratic National Convention in July,

CHAPTER FOUR

he talked about bringing the country together. He proclaimed, "There's not a **liberal** America and a **conservative** America. There's a United States of America." Obama won the election by a landslide.

During his three-year U.S. Senate career, Obama chose to tackle issues that brought Democrats and Republicans together. Meanwhile, his two **autobiographies** (aw-toh-by-AH-gruh-fees), *Dreams from My Father* and *The **Audacity** of Hope*, became bestsellers. He began to think about running for president.

Obama brought many Americans together during his presidential campaign. His catchy slogan, "Yes We Can," inspired voters to get involved. His internet-friendly campaign made the country seem close and connected. Americans could be "friends" with Obama on Facebook and MySpace. His website raised record-breaking funds when millions of people logged on to donate $10 or $20 at a time.

Obama's opponent was Senator John McCain of Arizona. A war veteran with 26 years in Congress, McCain pointed out Obama's lack

A POLITICAL STAR IS BORN

of experience with **foreign** (FAWR-in) governments. Obama responded by choosing Senator Joe Biden, an expert in foreign relations, to run as his vice president.

Some reporters pointed out the obvious—McCain was white, Obama was black. Would America elect a black president? Obama agreed that **racism** (RAY-sism) is real, but he argued, "If we simply retreat into our respective corners, we will never be able to come together and solve challenges like health care, or education, or the need to find good jobs for every American."

Election Day—November 4—brought record numbers of voters to the polls. That night, the winner was announced. It was Barack Obama!

Barack Obama and John McCain

President Obama signs the American Recovery and Reinvestment Act in Denver on February 17, 2009, while Vice President Joe Biden looks on.

Barack Obama is sworn in by Chief Justice John Roberts as the 44th President of the United States.

CHAPTER FIVE

"Yes We Can"

Barack Obama was sworn in as the 44th President on January 20, 2009. To symbolize how far both he and the country had come, he took his oath on Abraham Lincoln's Bible.

That January, Americans were struggling in the worst **recession** (ree-SEH-shun) since the 1930s. Tried-and-true U.S. companies such as automakers General Motors and Chrysler went bankrupt. By May 2009, more than 9 out of every 100 Americans had lost their jobs. Many people could not afford house payments and doctor's bills.

Obama's most important task became healing the wounded **economy** (ee-KAH-nuh-mee). He signed the American Recovery and Reinvestment Act less than a month after taking office. Promising to give $787 billion in

CHAPTER FIVE

government money to states, businesses, and individuals, this "**stimulus** bill" was based on Obama's campaign ideas. It included the largest tax cut in history to America's middle class. By the end of summer 2009, the economy was slowly turning around.

Next, Obama worked with Congress to figure out how they could help all Americans afford health care. Billions of dollars in Recovery Act money was set aside to hire more nurses and update old systems. Obama signed the CHIP bill on February 4, 2009. It would help pay medical bills for 4 million kids and pregnant women. Most important, he urged Congress to write a bill that would guarantee health care for all Americans, especially the millions left jobless by the recession.

Obama worked tirelessly to improve relations between the United States and other countries. His foreign policy differed greatly from that of the previous U.S. president, George W. Bush. Bush had hoped to protect America by refusing to work with its enemies. Obama instead encouraged all nations to think of the United States as a partner.

"YES WE CAN"

Obama's view was especially welcome in European and Islamic (is-LAH-mik) nations, who bitterly hated Bush's Iraq war. Obama

President Obama (center left), Italy's Prime Minister Silvio Berlusconi (top center), and Russia's President Dmitry Medvedev (center right) share a laugh as the leaders of the 20 richest nations in the world (the G20) pose for a group photo.

Other participants included Saudi Foreign Minister Prince Saud Al-Faisal (front left); Chinese President Hu Jintao (front center); British Prime Minister Gordon Brown (front right); Prime Minister of Turkey Recep Tayyip Erdogan (middle row left); South African President Kgalema Motlanthe (middle row right); Thailand's Prime Minister Abhisit Vejjajiva (top left); and Ethiopia's Prime Minister Meles Zenawi (top right). At this meeting, the G20 decided to give $1 trillion to help poor countries.

CHAPTER FIVE

reached out to Muslims worldwide in a June 2009 speech in Cairo, Egypt, when he quoted from three holy books: the Christian Bible, the Muslim Qur'an, and the Jewish Torah. He set a goal to do away with all nuclear weapons, and opened such talks with Iran, a longstanding U.S. enemy, and Russia.

On October 9, 2009, Obama's message of global cooperation (koh-ah-per-AY-shun) was rewarded with the Nobel Peace Prize. Past

President Obama met with Egyptian President Hosni Mubarak at the presidential palace in Cairo on June 4, 2009.

Mubarak had refused to talk with President George W. Bush, because he disapproved of the Iraq War. In 2009, Mubarak and Obama began to work together to encourage peace in the Middle East.

24

President Obama waves to the crowd at Cairo University in Egypt on June 4, 2009. During his speech there, he called for "a new beginning" between the U.S. and Islamic nations around the world.

CHAPTER FIVE

The Obamas—Barack, Sasha, Michelle, and Malia—pose for an official White House family portrait in October 2009.

winners include Martin Luther King Jr., Mother Theresa, and Nelson Mandela. The Nobel committee explained why they chose Obama for the award: "Only very rarely has a person . . . captured the world's attention and given its people hope for a better future." Now the world was listening to, and believing in, Obama's message of "Yes We Can."

CHRONOLOGY

1961 Barack Hussein Obama Jr. is born on August 4 to Barack Hussein Obama Sr. and Ann Dunham.

1963 Barack Obama Sr. attends Harvard on a scholarship, leaving Ann and two-year-old Barack in Hawaii. Ann later divorces him.

1967 Barack Jr., who is called Barry, moves to Indonesia with his mother and stepfather, Lelo Soetoro.

1971 Barry returns to Hawaii to live with grandparents; he attends the private Punahou School.

1979 He graduates from Punahou School and begins studies at Occidental College in Los Angeles.

1981 He transfers to Columbia University, where he will earn a degree in political science two years later.

1982 Barack Obama Sr. dies in a car crash in Kenya at age 46.

1985 Barack works as a community organizer on the South Side of Chicago.

1988 He enrolls in Harvard Law School.

1990 He is elected the first black president of *Harvard Law Review.*

1991 He graduates from Harvard Law School.

1992 Barack and Michelle Robinson marry in Chicago on October 3.

1995 His mother, Ann Dunham, dies of cancer at age 52.

1996 Barack is elected to Illinois State Senate.

1998 Barack and Michelle's daughter Malia Ann is born.

2000 Barack runs for the U.S. House of Representatives. He is defeated in the March primary by Bobby Rush.

2001 Barack and Michelle's daughter Natasha (Sasha) is born.

2004 Barack Obama is elected to the U.S. Senate.

2007 On February 10, he announces his run for the presidency.

2008 On November 4, he becomes first African American to win a presidential election.

2009 Barack Obama is sworn in as the 44th President of the United States on January 20. In October, he is honored with the Nobel Peace Prize.

TIMELINE IN HISTORY

1868 The Fourteenth Amendment secures citizenship rights for all Americans including African Americans.

1870 The Fifteenth Amendment guarantees voting rights for African American men.

1896 The Supreme Court says separate but equal facilities for blacks and whites are legal.

1909 The National Association for the Advancement of Colored People (NAACP) is organized.

1920s Millions of African Americans migrate from the South to the North in search of better job opportunities and less discrimination.

1929 The Great Depression begins in the United States.

1954 The Supreme Court says schools in the United States should be desegregated.

1963 Dr. Martin Luther King Jr. gives his "I Have a Dream" speech at the March on Washington for Jobs and Freedom in Washington, D.C.

1964 President Lyndon B. Johnson signs the Civil Rights Act of 1964.

1967 Thurgood Marshall becomes the first African American Supreme Court Justice.

1968 Civil rights activist Martin Luther King Jr. is assassinated in Memphis.

1981 Sandra Day O'Connor becomes the first female Supreme Court Justice.

2000 President William Jefferson Clinton signs the National Underground Railroad Freedom Center Act.

2006 Ceremonial groundbreaking takes place on the National Mall for the Dr. Martin Luther King, Jr., Memorial.

2007 Jamestown, Virginia, celebrates its 400th anniversary.

2009 Members of the Obama family become the first African American residents of the White House.

FIND OUT MORE

Books

Brophy, David Bergen. *Michelle Obama: Meet the First Lady.* New York: HarperCollins, 2009.

Edwards, Roberta. *Barack Obama: An American Story.* New York: Grosset & Dunlap, 2008.

Gormley, Beatrice. *Barack Obama: Our 44th President.* New York: Simon & Schuster, 2008.

Hughes, Libby. *Barack Obama: Voice of Unity, Hope, and Change.* Bloomington, IN: iUniverse.com, 2008.

Stier, Catherine. *If I Ran for President.* Morton Grove, IL: Albert Whitman & Company, 2007.

Thomas, Garen. *Yes We Can: A Biography of Barack Obama.* New York: Feiwel and Friends, 2008.

Winter, Jonah. *Barack.* New York: HarperCollins, 2008.

Works Consulted

The American Journey of Barack Obama. Ed. *Life Magazine.* New York: Little, Brown and Company, 2008.

Associated Press. "Illinois Sen. Barack Obama's Announcement Speech." *The Washington Post,* February 10, 2007.

Bates, Eric. "Barack Obama So Far." *Rolling Stone,* August 5, 2009. http://www.rollingstone.com/politics/story/29551986/barack_obama_so_far

CQ Transcripts Wire. "Sen. Barack Obama's Acceptance Speech in Chicago, Ill." *The Washington Post,* November 5, 2008.

Davey, Monica. "As Quickly as Overnight, a Democratic Star Is Born." *The New York Times,* March 18, 2004.

Dupuis, Martin, and Keith Boeckelman. *Barack Obama, the New Face of American Politics.* Westport, CT: Praeger Publishers, 2008.

Herbert, Bob. "A Leap of Faith." *The New York Times,* June 4, 2004.

Huffington Post. "Obama's Speech in Cairo." June 4, 2009. http://www.huffingtonpost.com/2009/06/04/obama-speech-in-cairo-vid_n_211215.html

Kovaleski, Serge. "Obama's Organizing Years, Guiding Others, Finding Himself." *The New York Times,* July 7, 2008. http://www.nytimes.com/2008/07/07/us/politics/07community.html

Mendell, David. *Obama: From Promise to Power.* New York: HarperCollins, 2007.

Mundy, Liza. *Michelle.* New York: Simon & Schuster, 2008.

Murray, Mark. " 'Rock Star' Obama in the Land of Lincoln." MSNBC.com, February 10, 2007. http://www.msnbc.msn.com/id/17086451

Norwegian Nobel Committee, The. "The Nobel Peace Prize 2009—Press Release." October 9, 2009. http://nobelprize.org/nobel_prizes/peace/laureates/2009/press.html

FIND OUT MORE

Obama, Barack. *The Audacity of Hope.* New York: Crown Publishers, 2006.
———. *Change We Can Believe In.* New York: Three Rivers Press, 2008.
———. *Dreams from My Father.* New York: Crown Publishers, 1995.
———. "What I Want for You—And Every Child in America." *Parade Magazine,* January 18, 2009. http://www.parade.com/export/sites/default/news/2009/01/barack-obama-letter-to-my-daughters.html
Page, Susan. "Hurdles Remain in Obama's Push to Revamp Health Care." *USA Today,* June 1, 2009.
Saslow, Eli. "The Prize and the Presidency: Reactions Similar Only in Their Intensity." *The Washington Post,* October 10, 2009. http://www.washingtonpost.com/wp-dyn/content/story/2009/10/09/ST2009100901112.html?sid=ST2009100901112
Scott, Janny. "A Free-Spirited Wanderer Who Set Obama's Path." *The New York Times,* March 14, 2008. http://www.nytimes.com/2008/03/14/us/politics/14obama.html
———. "Obama's Account of New York Years Often Differs From What Others Say." *New York Times,* October 30, 2007. http://www.nytimes.com/2007/10/30/us/politics/30obama.html
Shunk, Chris. "Obama Signs Cash-for-Clunkers Bill into Law, Countdown to Start Begins." *Autoblog Green,* June 26, 2009. http://green.autoblog.com/2009/06/26/obama-signs-cash-for-clunkers-bill-into-law-countdown-to-start
United States Department of Labor. "Employment Situation Summary." October 2, 2009. http://www.bls.gov/news.release/empsit.nr0.htm

On the Internet
If You Were President
http://teacher.scholastic.com/scholasticnews/games_quizzes/electiongame/game.asp
Rosenbloom, Jonathan. "Obama Wins Nobel Peace Prize," *Time for Kids,* October 9, 2009. http://www.timeforkids.com/TFK/kids/news/story/0,28277,1929432,00.html
Speak Out
http://pbskids.org/speakout/
Time for Kids Election '08
http://www.timeforkids.com/TFK/election08/cand_obama.html
White House
http://www.whitehouse.gov

Photo Credits: Cover, pp. 1, 3, 8, 11, 12, 15, 16, 20, 26, 27, 28—WhiteHouse.gov; p. 4 (top)—Mark Wilson/Getty Images; p. 4 (bottom)—Scout Tufankjian; p. 6—America.gov; p. 23—Press Assocation/AP Images; pp. 24, 25—Mandel Ngan/AFP/Getty Images. Every effort has been made to locate all copyright holders of material used in this book. If any errors or omissions have occurred, corrections will be made in future editions of the book.

GLOSSARY

apartheid (uh-PAR-tyd)—A government policy in South Africa to keep races separate, or apart; the policy was in place from 1948 to 1994.
audacity (aw-DAA-sih-tee)—Shocking boldness; extreme daring.
autobiography (aw-toh-by-AH-gruh-fee)—The story of someone's life, told by that person.
campaign (kam-PAYN)—An effort to convince people to vote for someone or something.
community (kuh-MYOO-nih-tee)—A group of people living together.
conservative (con-SER-vuh-tiv)—Favoring traditional views and values.
diffuse (dih-FYOOZ)—To make safer; to make something less likely to explode.
economy (ee-KAH-nuh-mee)—The way a government and businesses work together to provide people who buy things with the goods and services they want.
exotic (ek-ZAH-tik)—Different or unusual.
foreign (FAWR-in)—From another country.
heritage (HAYR-ih-tidj)—Something passed down in a person's family.
internship (IN-turn-ship)—A job done for experience instead of for money.
liberal (LIB-rul)—Favoring proposals for reform, open to new ideas for progress, and tolerant of the ideas and behavior of others.
minorities (my-NAHR-ih-teez)—Groups of people whose race or opinions differ from those of most of a population.
obstacle (OB-stih-kul)—Something that stands in the way.
philosophy (fih-LAH-suh-fee)—The study of thoughts and ideas.
pitch—Black tarlike material used for building and paving roads.
racism (RAY-sism)—The belief that a person thinks or acts a certain way, or deserves certain things, because of his or her race.
recession (ree-SEH-shun)—A period of time when businesses struggle, forcing many workers out of their jobs.
scholarship (SKAH-lur-ship)—Money awarded to exceptional students, usually to help pay for school.
stimulus (STIH-myoo-lus)—Something that gets something else moving.

INDEX

American Recovery and Reinvestment Act 20, 21–22
Biden, Joe 19, 20
Boyer, John 13
Bush, George W. 6, 22, 23
Chicago 14, 15, 17
Chicago, University of 12
CHIP bill 22
Columbia University 13
Democratic National Convention 16, 17–18
Democrats 6, 18
Dunham, Stanley and Madelyn 10, 12
Dunham, Stanley Ann 8, 9–10
Economy 7
Egypt 24, 25
Elections
    Presidential, 2004 5–6
    Presidential, 2008 4, 5–7, 18–19
    State Senate, 1996 17
    U.S. Representative, 2000 17
    U.S. Senate, 2004 4, 16, 17–18
G20 23
Harvard Law Review 14
Harvard University 9, 14
Hawaii 9–11
Health care 4, 7, 17, 19, 22
Illinois State Senate 5, 16, 17
Indonesia 10
Internet 18
Iraq War 4, 6, 23, 24
Islamic nations 23, 24, 25
Lincoln, Abraham 5, 21
McCain, John 18–19
New York City 13
Nobel Peace Prize 24, 26
Nuclear weapons 24
Obama, Barack Hussein, Sr. 8, 9
Obama, Barack Hussein, Jr.
    books authored by 18
    childhood of 8, 9–11
    children of 17, 26
    as community organizer 14
    education of 10–11, 13–14
    offices held 5, 16, 17–18, 20, 21–26
    as professor 13
Obama, Malia 17, 26
Obama, Michelle Robinson 15, 17, 26
Obama, Natasha 17, 26
Occidental College 13
Punahou School 10–11
Racism 19
Recession 21, 22
Republicans 6, 18
Roberts, John 20
Rush, Bobby 17
Sidley Austin 14
Slavery 5
Soetoro, Lelo 10
Soetoro-Ng, Maya 10, 11
U.S. Senate 16, 17, 18
Washington, Harold 14

SEP 2 2 2010

25⁷⁰